DATE DUE

DATE DUE

THE Pilgrims Knew

THE Pilgrims

Knew

BY TILLIE S. PINE
and JOSEPH LEVINE

Pictures by Ezra Jack Keats

McGraw-Hill Book Company

New York   Toronto   London

Also by Tillie S. Pine and Joseph Levine

THE CHINESE KNEW

THE EGYPTIANS KNEW

THE ESKIMOS KNEW

THE INDIANS KNEW

AIR ALL AROUND

ELECTRICITY AND HOW WE USE IT

FRICTION ALL AROUND

GRAVITY ALL AROUND

HEAT ALL AROUND

LIGHT ALL AROUND

MAGNETS AND HOW WE USE THEM

SIMPLE MACHINES AND HOW WE USE THEM

SOUNDS ALL AROUND

WATER ALL AROUND

WEATHER ALL AROUND

When the Pilgrims landed on our shores over three hundred years ago, they found thick forests, rushing streams, animals and plants of many kinds.

They hunted, they fished, they planted.

They built their own homes, they made their own clothing.

They knew

How to make windows without using glass

How to make wind and moving water work for them

How to spin thread and weave cloth

How to make candles and soap

How to make maple syrup and sugar

How to get oil from seeds

You will find out that the Pilgrims knew how to make use of what they found around them, just as many people did everywhere.

You will see how they were able to make a home for themselves in their new and strange land.

The Pilgrims knew

how to make moving air work for them.
They put sails on the ships they built.
The wind blew against the sails and moved the ships.
The ship that brought the Pilgrims to our shores in
the year 1620 was a sailing ship, the *Mayflower*.
The Pilgrims also used windmills.
The arms of the windmills, moved by the wind,
turned wheels inside the mill
which ground the corn kernels into flour.

Today

people in many parts of the world still use the wind to drive sailboats and windmills.

High-flying planes make use of fast-moving winds which blow over the earth.

By flying along with the winds, the planes go faster.

You

can see that moving air can move things.

Make a paper pinwheel.

Draw crosslines to the opposite corners of a square piece of paper.

Cut along these lines to an inch from the center of the paper.

Fold corners 1, 2, 3, and 4 to the center.

Put a pin through these ends and the center.

Fasten the pin to a stick.

Hold the pinwheel in the wind.

Blow on it.

Watch it turn!

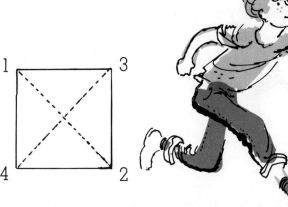

The Pilgrims knew

how to make moving water work for them.
They used fast-moving streams to turn their water wheels.
They ground corn and other grains in their water mills.
The Pilgrims built the first water mill in our country
in the year 1633.

Today

we use moving water to make electricity.
The water flowing over a dam hits the paddles
of a giant water wheel, called a turbine.
The water wheel whirls around and turns a big machine.
As the machine turns, it makes electricity.
The electricity goes through wires to homes and factories.

You

can see that moving water can move things.
Cut several slits into the edge of the cover of an
oatmeal box.   Insert a two-inch piece of cardboard in
each slit.
Push a pencil through the center of the cover.   Hold both
ends of the pencil lightly and let running water from a
faucet hit the cardboard paddles.
Watch the running water turn your water wheel
around and around.

The Pilgrims knew

how to make candles from tallow and from wax.
They saved and melted hard fat, called tallow, which
they cut from bear, deer, and moose meat.
They picked and boiled the berry of the bayberry bush
to get wax.
The wicks for the candles were made from loosely spun cotton.
The Pilgrims dipped the wicks
into the melted tallow or wax
to coat them.
They did this over and over again until they made the
candles the size they wanted.
The Pilgrims also made candles by pouring the melted
tallow or wax into candle molds.

Today

most of our candles are molded in factories.
Some are hand-dipped.
We, too, use wicks of cotton.
Instead of animal fat, we use paraffin wax taken from
wood, coal, or oil.
Bright dyes are added to the wax to color the candles.

You

can make a candle.
Ask a grownup to melt paraffin wax in a double boiler.
This wax is usually used to seal jars of jelly.
Dip a string into the melted wax.
Remove the string and allow the wax on it to harden.
Do this many times.
Make a thin candle.
Make a fat candle.

The Pilgrims knew

how to make soap.
They made lye from wood ashes, straw, lime, and water.
They boiled the lye with animal fat until the
mixture became soap.
They used this soap in their washing.

Today

many different kinds of soap are made for cleaning and
washing.
Some soaps are still made of fat and lye—the same
materials that the Pilgrims used.
The fat and the lye are boiled
in large vats in factories.
Bar, liquid, and powdered soaps are made.
Sometimes colors and perfumes are added to make the soap
attractive and sweet-smelling.

You

are not going to make soap, because lye is
dangerous to handle.
But—
You can see that dirt can be washed away better with
soap than without soap.
Rub two pieces of white cloth in dirt.
Wash one in clear water.
Wash the other in soapy water.
You will see how the soap
has helped to wash the dirt away.

The Pilgrims knew

how to get oil from seeds.
They crushed the seeds of the flax plant to get the oil.
They used this oil in their cooking.

Today

machines crush cotton seeds, peanuts, soybeans, and other kinds of seeds and nuts to get the oil.

Mother uses these oils in salads, in cooking, and in baking.

You

can see that there is oil in nuts, which are seeds.

Shell a walnut, a peanut, or an almond.

Rub the inside of the nut meat on a piece of brown paper.

When you see a grease spot
where you are rubbing,
you will know that the oil in the nut
made the spot.

The Pilgrims knew

that heat travels.

On cold winter nights, the Pilgrim mothers put hot coals into metal warming pans.

Before the children went to bed, the warming pans were moved around between the cold sheets.

The heat of the hot coals traveled through the metal pans and warmed up the bed.

Today

we burn coal or oil in a furnace to boil water into steam.
The steam travels through pipes from the furnace to the
radiators in our rooms.
The hot radiators warm the air, and the air warms us.

You

can find out that heat travels.
Put a metal teaspoon into a cup of hot water.
After a few minutes, notice that the handle of the
spoon has become warm.   The heat has traveled
through the metal spoon to your fingers.
You can also find out that heat travels through the air.
Hold your hands in front of a warm radiator and feel the
heat as it travels from the radiator, through the air,
to your hands.

The Pilgrims knew

how to make maple syrup and maple sugar.
They went into the forest in the early spring to
find maple trees.
They made deep cuts in the bark of these trees and put
wooden spouts in the cuts.
The sap in the trees dripped into buckets.
The Pilgrims then boiled the sap in large open pots over
an outdoor fire. As the water in the sap evaporated, the
sap thickened into syrup.
When they wanted to make sugar, they boiled the sap
longer to evaporate more of the water.

Today

we make maple syrup and maple sugar
very much the same way the Pilgrims did.
We use maple syrup in cooking.
We pour maple syrup over pancakes and waffles.
We also make maple-sugar candy.

You

can make syrup.
Dissolve about four tablespoons of sugar in a cup of water.
You might call this sugar-water the "sap."
Boil the "sap" slowly in a saucepan.
As the water evaporates, the liquid thickens
into sugar-syrup.
You can use this syrup to sweeten a dish of berries.

19

The Pilgrims knew

how to use flint and steel to make sparks.
They struck a sharp, hard stone, called flint, against
a piece of steel.
Sparks flew!
They made the sparks fall on some partly burned linen
kept in a "tinder" box.
"Tinder" is a name for anything that catches fire easily.
The Pilgrims used the lighted tinder to start their fires.

Today

we use flint and steel in most cigarette lighters.
When the small steel wheel of the cigarette lighter is
turned, the wheel rubs against a piece of flint.
Sparks fly and set fire to the oily wick.
Welders also use a long flint-and-steel spark maker to
light their torches.   The spark maker is safer to use than
matches.

You

can make sparks fly by hitting a piece of metal sharply
against a hard rock.
Sometimes, you can see sparks fly when a roller skater,
skating fast, turns suddenly on the sidewalk.   The steel
wheels of the skates rub against the stony sidewalk
and cause sparks to fly.

21

The Pilgrims knew

that air keeps fire burning.
When they started fires in their large fireplaces, they blew
air into the fires with bellows until the fires burned brightly.
The Pilgrim blacksmith also used bellows to make
his fires hot enough to shape iron into the things
he wanted to make.

Today

furnaces in homes, in shops, in factories, and in ships are
built with air openings at the bottom to allow
fresh air to enter.
The air keeps the fires burning.

You

can see that air keeps fire burning.
Drip a little wax from a short lighted candle into a dish.
Stand the candle in the hot wax.
Place a glass, top down, over the burning candle.
The flame will soon go out because the glass keeps
fresh air away from the flame.

The Pilgrims knew

how to make butter.
After milking their cows,
they poured some of the milk
into large deep pans.
The next day, they took off
the thick cream which had risen
to the top of the milk.
They poured the cream into a churn
and moved the "dasher"
up and down in the churn
until the cream thickened into butter.
Some of the butter was salted
so that it could be kept a long time
without spoiling.

Today

machines help us make most of our butter.
Electric "separators" take the cream from the milk.
Huge churns turn the cream into butter.
The butter is shaped and packaged by other machines.

You

can make butter.
Pour some heavy cream into a deep dish.
This cream already has been "separated."
Whip the cream with a fork or an egg beater until the
cream thickens into butter.
Use the butter on some biscuits or bread.

The Pilgrims knew

that food could be kept from spoiling
by salting, drying, spicing, pickling,
smoking, or cooling it.
They salted meat and fish.
They dried fruits.
They spiced meats.
They pickled vegetables.
They smoked beef, ham, and bacon.
They cooled butter.

Today

we have many ways of keeping food from spoiling.
We spice, dry, salt, pickle, and smoke different foods,
as the Pilgrims did.
We have many other ways of preserving foods.
We cool foods in refrigerators to keep them from spoiling.
We freeze foods to keep them for a long time.
We can foods.

You

can prove that milk can be kept from spoiling by cooling it.
Place a small jar of milk in the refrigerator.
Keep another small jar of milk on the kitchen shelf.
After several days, notice which milk is still fresh and
which has spoiled.

The Pilgrims knew

how to spin thread and weave cloth.
They spun cotton thread from the cotton plant.
They spun linen thread from the flax plant.
They spun wool yarn from the wool of sheep.
The Pilgrim women spun these threads on
spinning wheels and wove them into cloth
on hand looms.
Sometimes, they wove linen and wool threads into a
rough, strong cloth which they called linsey-woolsey.

Today

we spin cotton, linen, wool, and silk threads.
We also have learned how to make new kinds of thread
like nylon and rayon.
We dye these threads and weave them into many different kinds
of cloth.

You

can find out how cloth is woven.
Make a simple hand loom from a piece of cardboard or
an old picture frame.
You can buy a toy loom, if you wish.
Use cord or wool yarn as your thread.
Weave this thread into a mat on your loom.

The Pilgrims knew

how to make windows without using glass.
They used oiled paper or cloth.
They rubbed fat or oil on paper or cloth, which they put
over the window openings of their houses.
The oiled paper or cloth allowed light to go through.
However, no one could see through these "windows."
The Pilgrims did not use glass in their windows for
many years because they did not make their own glass
and because it cost too much to bring it from England.

Today

we make windows using clear glass.
Glass is made in large factories.
It is cheap enough for everyone to use.

You

can prove that oiled paper lets more light go through than
unoiled paper.
Hold a piece of brown wrapping paper in front of a window.
See how it shuts out most of the light.
Now rub a little butter or oil on a part of the paper.
Hold the paper up to the light again.
You will see that more light comes through the oiled part
than through the unoiled part.

You have read about some of the things that the Pilgrims knew and did when they settled in their new homeland.

You have found out that we do many things that the Pilgrims did.

But—

Today we use machines run by electricity to help us!

We use huge looms in large mills to weave our cloth.

We use large churns in dairies to make butter.

We use furnaces to heat our buildings.

When you grow up, you will still do many things that the Pilgrims did.

And—

There will be newer and different ways of doing these same things.

D